SELECTIONS FROM

FANTASTIC BEASTS

AND WHERE TO FIND THEM

ORIGINAL SCORE COMPOSED BY
JAMES NEWTON HOWARD

Produced by
Alfred Music
P.O. Box 10003
Van Nuys, CA 91410-0003
alfred.com

Printed in USA.

No part of this book shall be reproduced, arranged, adapted, recorded, publicly performed, stored in a retrieval system, or transmitted by any means without written permission from the publisher. In order to comply with copyright laws, please apply for such written permission and/or license by contacting the publisher at alfred.com/permissions.

ISBN-10: 1-4706-3824-X
ISBN-13: 978-1-4706-3824-5

Album art direction: Sandeep Sriram
Scoring photos by Benjamin Ealovega

Easy Piano arrangements by Dan Coates

CONTENTS

MAGICAL CONGRESS OF THE UNITED STATES OF AMERICA

NEWT SAYS GOODBYE TO TINA/
JACOB'S BAKERY

(from *Fantastic Beasts and Where to Find Them*)

Composed by James Newton Howard
Arr. Dan Coates

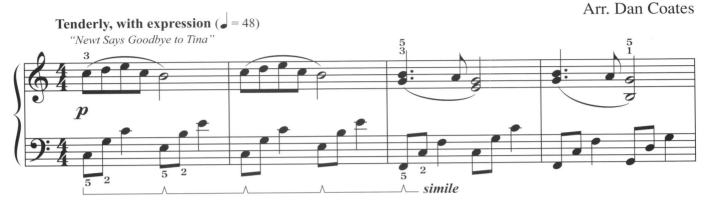

Moderate swing (♩ = 110) (♫ = ♩♪)
"Jacob's Bakery"

Slower (♩ = 92) (♫ = ♩♪)

A MAN AND HIS BEASTS

(from *Fantastic Beasts and Where to Find Them*)

Composed by James Newton Howard
Arr. Dan Coates

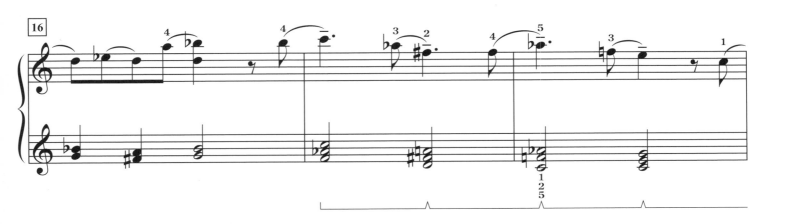

A little faster (♩ = 112)

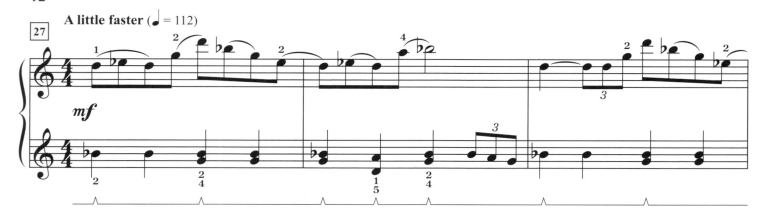

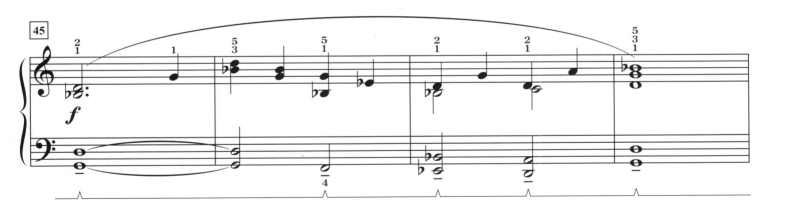

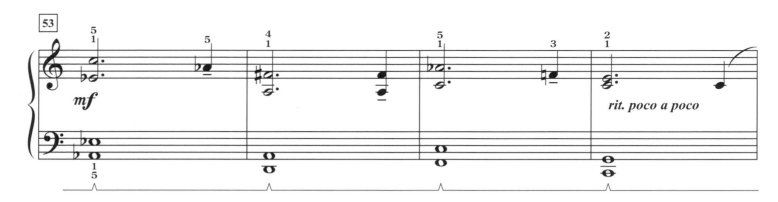

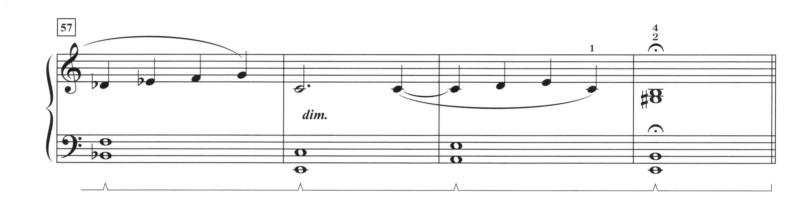

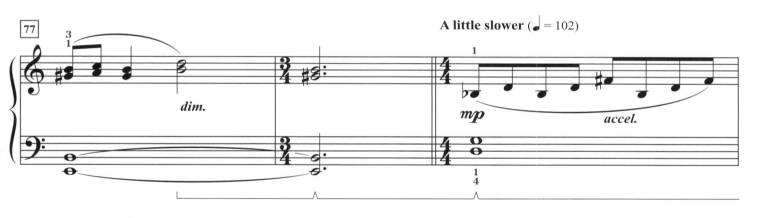

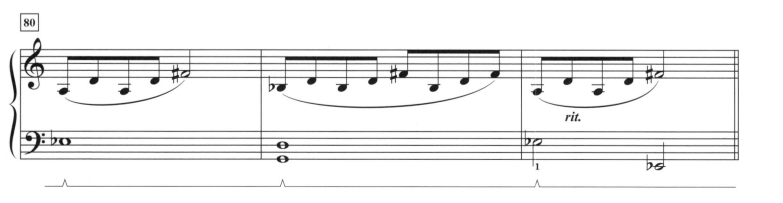

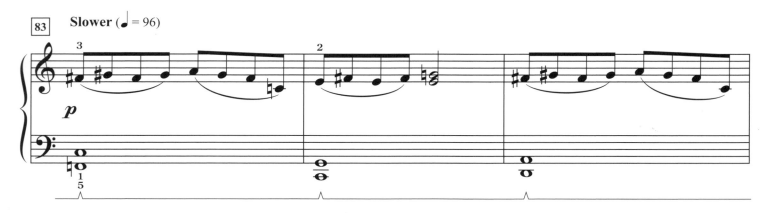

A little slower (♩ = 91)

Special Feed Codes

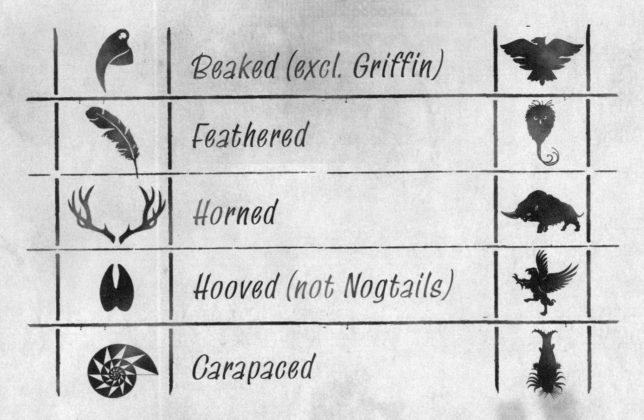

Beaked (excl. Griffin)	
Feathered	
Horned	
Hooved (not Nogtails)	
Carapaced	

Habitat & Terrain Codes

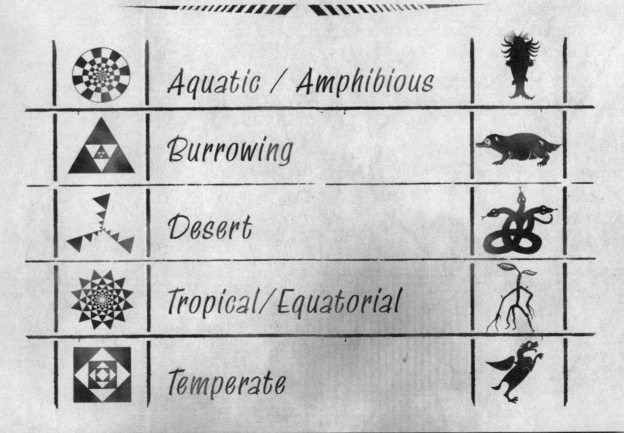

Aquatic / Amphibious	
Burrowing	
Desert	
Tropical/Equatorial	
Temperate	

BLIND PIG
(from *Fantastic Beasts and Where to Find Them*)

Written by J. K. Rowling and Mario Grigorov
Arr. Dan Coates

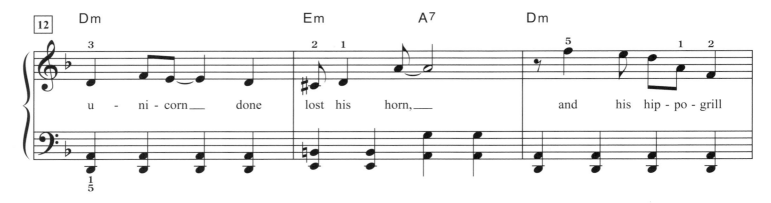

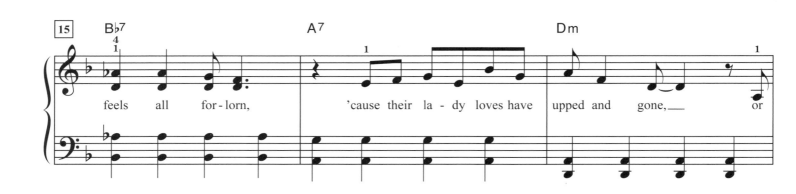

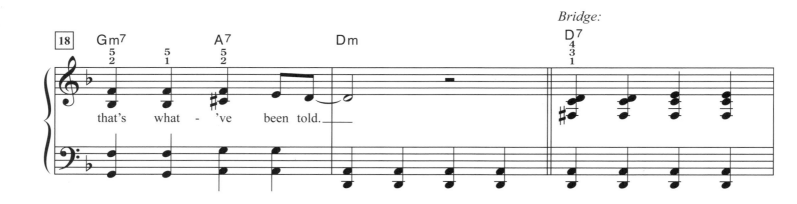

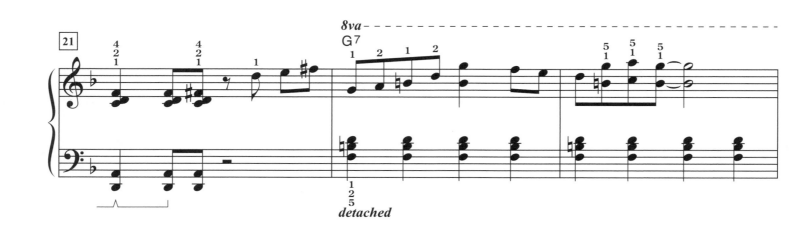

21

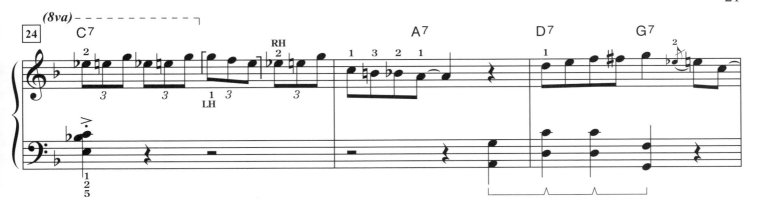

2. Yes,____ love,____ love has set the____ beasts a - stir.

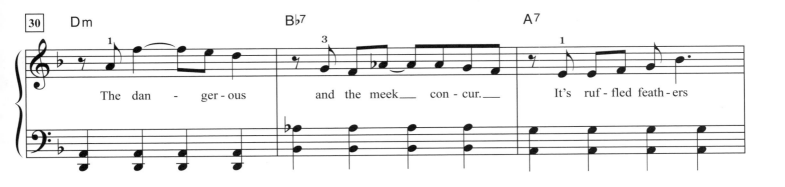

The dan - ger - ous____ and the meek____ con - cur.____ It's ruf - fled feath - ers

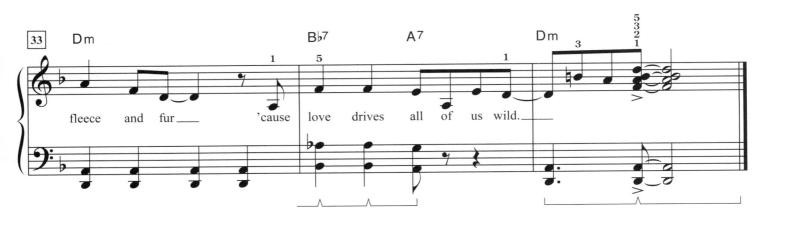

fleece and fur____ 'cause love drives all of us wild.____

END TITLES PT. 2

(from *Fantastic Beasts and Where to Find Them*)

Composed by James Newton Howard
Arr. Dan Coates

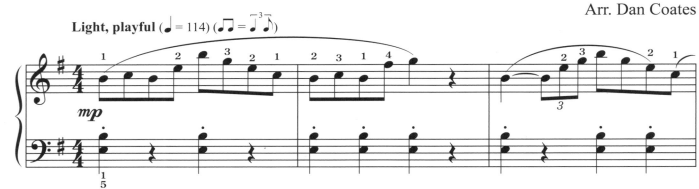

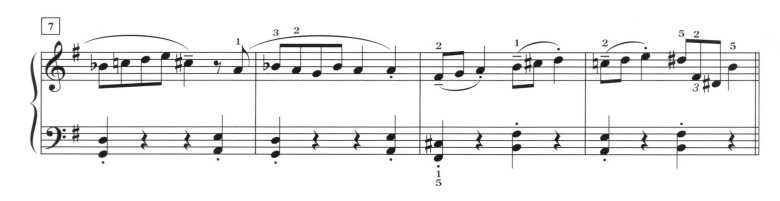

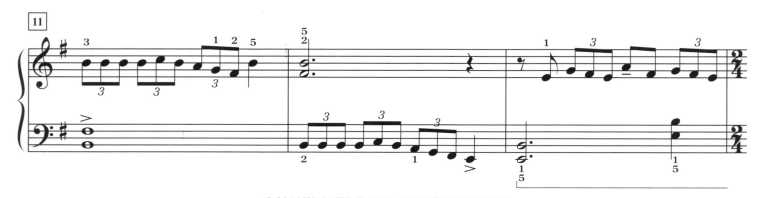

KOWALSKI RAG

(from *Fantastic Beasts and Where to Find Them*)

Composed by James Newton Howard
Arr. Dan Coates

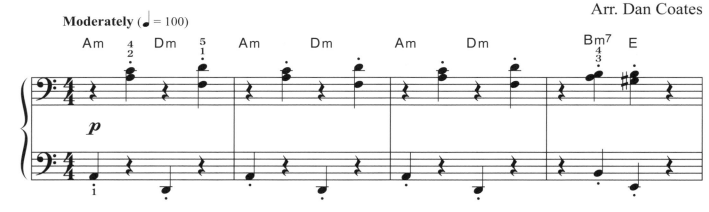

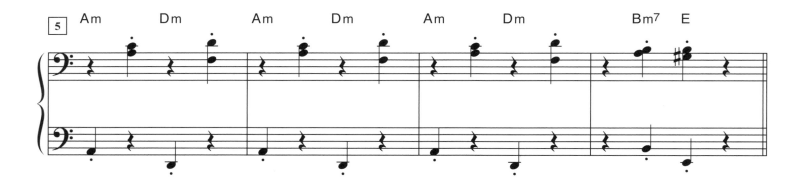

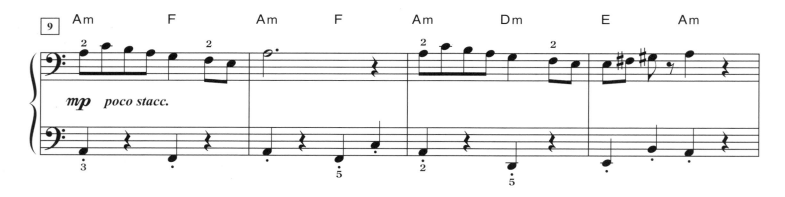

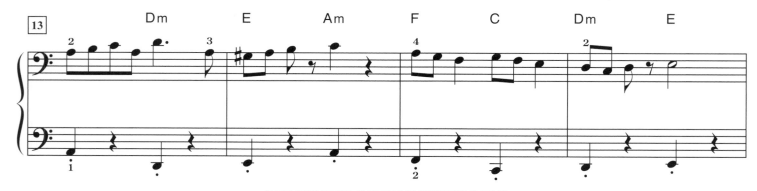

29